Upon the Stair

Tales from *The Book of Darkness & Light*

by Adam Z. Robinson

Stories

The Cry of the Bubák

Mirrorman

The Xylotheque

Upon the Stair is a co-production between The Book of Darkness & Light, Harrogate Theatre, Square Chapel Arts Centre and LittleMighty.

Published by Playdead Press 2022

© Adam Z. Robinson 2022

Adam Z. Robinson has asserted his rights under the Copyright, Design and Patents Act, 1988, to be identified as the author of this work.

A CIP catalogue record for this book is available from the British Library.

ISBN 978-1-915533-03-6

Caution

Playdead Press
www.playdeadpress.com

Cover design: Wayne Gamble
Photography: Barnaby Aldrick
Set design: Emma Williams

For Carol
and for every inspiring English teacher

CAST & CREATIVE TEAM

Adam Z. Robinson | Writer and 'The Storyteller'

Dick Bonham | Director

Raphaella Julien | 'The Shade'

Chloe Hayward | Composer and 'The Musician'

Lynsey Jones | Voice of 'Tippi'

Jeni Draper | Dramaturg

Brian Duffy | BSL Consultant and VV Advisor

Adam Bassett | BSL Consultant and VV Advisor

Emma Williams | Set and Costume Designer

Tim Skelly | Lighting Designer

Guy Connelly | Sound Designer

Matt Sykes-Hooban | Technical Stage Manager

LittleMighty | Producer

CAST AND CREATIVE TEAM BIOGRAPHIES

ADAM Z. ROBINSON | WRITER AND 'THE STORYTELLER'

Adam Z. Robinson is a writer, performer and theatre-maker. His play *The Book of Darkness & Light* ("Truly remarkable... Stunningly scary... Unmissable." – Great British Ghosts) toured extensively in 2016-18. The play has subsequently been produced by theatre companies in Canada and Australia. Adam's follow-up show, *Shivers* ("Kept me enthralled from the very beginning" – British Theatre Guide), toured the UK in 2018-19 to more than 30 theatres. Both plays are published by Playdead Press. In 2021 Adam was commissioned by The Dukes, Lancaster, to write *Belle and Mary*, a true crime play based on historical events. The show premiered in November 2021. Adam's adaptation of Charles Dickens' *A Christmas Carol* toured nationally in December 2019 and 2021. Adam wrote *Smile Club* (★★★★ The Guardian) with Andrea Heaton, a dystopian drama produced by Red Ladder Theatre Company. The play premiered at the Leeds Playhouse in March 2020 before touring. Adam's other writing work includes: *Conscientious* (national tour 2014), *Seaside Terror* (with Odd Doll Theatre, toured 2017-20) and short film *The Split* (dir. Ed Rigg, starring Edward Hogg). www.adamzrobinson.com

DICK BONHAM | DIRECTOR

Dick Bonham is an experienced director and dramaturg. He was dramaturg on *The Book of Darkness & Light*, *Shivers* and directed the company's adaptation of *A Christmas Carol*. His other work includes directing Dan Bye's Fringe First Award winning *Going Viral*, as well as previous pieces *The Price of Everything* and *How to Occupy An Oil Rig*. Other projects include Matthew Bellwood's *An Icy Man* (Leeds Playhouse) and Emma Decent's *Beyond Dreams of Aberystwyth*. He wrote and directed Sometimes We Play's *We Can Be Heroes* (national tour 2015). He wrote Common Chorus Theatre's *If I Say Jump* and is currently collaborating with Simon Brewis on *The Ghost of Stolen Summer*, commissioned by Harrogate Theatre and premiering in 2023.

RAPHAELLA JULIEN | 'THE SHADE'
Raphaella Julien is a professional Deaf dancer, actor, BSL Director and Movement Director from Manchester. She was born profoundly Deaf. Her credits include: Weft in *The Emperor's New Clothes* (Derby Theatre/Polka Theatre), Gem in *Treasure Island* (Derby Theatre), Ismene in *Antigone* (Storyhouse Theatre, Chester), Cathy 2 in *The Last 5 Years* (Welsh Tour), The Who's *Tommy* (UK Tour), Amy in *Trinity* (Tilt Films), Esther in *Jerk* (Rough-cut TV), Molly in *Hunch* (Reid Productions), Heather in *Clink* (Channel 5), Friend in *Sweetstake* (Mars Bar commercial), Deviser, Collaborator and Light Blue in *Night Shift* (ZooCo), BSL Director *The Hunchback of Notre Dame* (NYMT), BSL Presenter/Narrator *Josephine* (The Egg, Bath), Movement Director *Antigone* (Storyhouse Theatre, Chester), BSL Consultant *Stan* (Art with Heart). As dancer: *The International Dance Show* (Cyprus), *The Michael Jackson Show* (Crete), *More than Words* (MNEK Music Video - Warner Records), *The Dorm-Room* (Music Video for Suli Breaks), Dancer and Narrator in *Vogue Ball Documentary*. In 2022, Raphaella won the Deaffest Best Actress Award for her role in short film *Lost, Taken, Murdered*.

CHLOE HAYWARD | COMPOSER AND 'THE MUSICIAN'
Chloe Hayward is a professional freelance violinist who graduated from Leeds Conservatoire with a degree in

Classical Music. As a performer, Chloe has played with groups such as VOCI String Quartet, The Untold Orchestra, Urban Soul Orchestra, The Northern Opera Group, Gatecrasher Classical Orchestra, Ignition Orchestra, London String Group, Northern Film Orchestra and The Yorkshire Symphony Orchestra. Chloe previously worked as a teaching artist for Opera North and also currently works within community music settings for Songbirds Music and Made with Music. Chloe works for WMP as a fixer and violinist, playing on tracks used for TV and advertising. Chloe is also a member of the band VRAELL. Chloe has worked with The Book of Darkness & Light as the musician and composer for *A Christmas Carol* and *Upon The Stair.*

LYNSEY JONES | VOICE OF 'TIPPI'

Lynsey Jones trained with Red Ladder Theatre Company in 2010. Since then, she has worked extensively with Red Ladder, taking lead roles in *Promised Land* (2012) and *Leeds Lads* (2016). More recently she toured with Common Chorus Theatre in their physical theatre show *Drink with a Chimp* (2015) and *If I Say Jump* (2018). Lynsey also co-directs Suitcase and Spectacles Theatre Company and tours their one woman show *Miss Dotty's Specs* (2019) to local audiences in Leeds.

JENI DRAPER | DRAMATURG

Jeni Draper is the Artistic Director of fingersmiths, a physical theatre company working with Deaf and hearing actors performing in BSL and spoken English. The company delivers a range of training courses including Deaf Awareness Training and consultancy services for theatres, artists and arts organisations. Jeni is also a qualified sign language interpreter specialising in theatre. As director, her theatre credits include *My Mother Said I Never Should* (Sheffield Crucible and tour), *Up 'n' Under* (New Wolsey Theatre and tour), *Frozen* (Birmingham Rep co-production) and *War Crimes for the Home* (tour).

BRIAN DUFFY | BSL CONSULTANT AND VV ADVISOR

Brian Duffy is an actor both on stage and TV. He collaborated with Elf Lyons on *HEIST* at Soho Theatre. Brian is the co-creator and co-writer of sign language sitcom *Small World*. He previously worked on *4.48 Psychosis* by Sarah Kane. He collaborated with a Deaf Persian actor and produced *NuVisual*, in the styles of traditional mime and VV. Brian has worked with The Globe and the Royal Shakespeare Company with translations from Shakespeare to BSL. He worked as BSL consultant on the Sky series *I Hate Suzie* by Bad Wolf. He assistant-directed *The Process* with Baz Productions, as well working on a musical *Here/Not Here* with Bim Ajadi / Artemisia Films.

ADAM BASSETT | BSL CONSULTANT AND VV ADVISOR

Adam Bassett is from Kingston-upon-Hull. His acting short film credits include *Retreat*, *Four Deaf Yorkshiremen Go to Blackpool*, *Deaf Funny* as well as starring in the BSL Zone sitcom *Small World*. Adam also appeared in the BBC's *Moving On*. In theatre, Adam appeared in *Love's Labour's Lost*, *A Midsummer Night's Dream* and *4.48 Psychosis* with Deafinitely Theatre, *Up 'n 'Under* with fingersmiths and *Macbeth* with Leeds Playhouse. In street theatre, he was involved in WRAS's *The Best of all Possible Worlds* tour. As a BSL consultant, Adam worked with The Book of Darkness & Light on *Upon the Stair*, *Dare Master* (CITV) and *A Christmas Carol* with Leeds Playhouse. Adam was Associate Director on Ramps on the Moon's *Oliver Twist*. Adam is a presenter on

BSL Zone's *The Muddy Boot Room* and Zebra Uno's *Deaffest: Rewind*. Adam also appears on-screen for ITV's Signpost productions.

EMMA WILLIAMS | SET AND COSTUME DESIGNER

Emma Williams is a set and costume designer. She trained at Wimbledon School of Art and her designs have been predominantly for new and emerging work. Some of her ground-breaking and critically acclaimed shows include: *Refugee Boy, Queen of Chapeltown, You The Player, Two Tracks and Text Me* and *Scuffer*, all for Leeds Playhouse; *Everything I Own* and *Abigail's Party* for Hull Truck Theatre; *Smile Club* (by Adam Z. Robinson and Andrea Heaton) for Red Ladder; *Iyalode of Eti* for Utopia Theatre; *Belle and Mary* (by Adam Z. Robinson) and *The Slow Songs Make Me Sad*, both for The Dukes Lancaster.

TIM SKELLY | LIGHTING DESIGNER

Tim Skelly is a lighting designer for performance and exhibition and an educator who teaches theatre and performance design at the University of Salford. Recent credits include: *Blake Remixed* (LittleMighty), *Whisker's First Winter* (Odd Doll), *One Man Two Guvnors* (Derby Theatre), *Berlin to Broadway* (Opera North), *Merchant of Venice* (Stafford Shakespeare Festival), *Around the World in 80 Days* and *Be My Baby* (Leeds Playhouse), and *The Damned United* (Red Ladder Theatre Company).

GUY CONNELLY | SOUND DESIGNER

Guy Connelly is a composer, sound designer, songwriter and music producer. He has scored/sound-designed over 35 shows for theatre and dance including: *Butterflies, Home, One Million* and *Care* with Tangled Feet; *Back to the Future* and *Miller's Crossing* for Secret Cinema; *The Dan Daw Show* for Dan Daw; *What Once Was Ours* and *Youthquake* with Zest Theatre (winner Best Production for Young People 13+ Off West End Awards 2018); *Off The Grid* and *Crowded* with Half Moon Theatre (Best Production for Young People 13+ Off West End Awards 2019). Other composition includes commissions for BBC, Channel 4, Sky, NBC, Fox, Rambert Dance, Alexander Whitley Dance Company, and the V&A. As Clock Opera, Guy has released three acclaimed albums, toured the world and remixed Christine and The Queens, Feist, Metronomy, Everything Everything, Charlotte Gainsbourg, Tracey Thorn, Marina & The Diamonds, and many more.

MATT SYKES-HOOBAN | TECHNICAL STAGE MANAGER

Matt Sykes-Hooban works as a freelance technical production manager around the UK and further afield. Recent projects include *Whisker's First Winter* for Odd Doll Puppetry Theatre and *Wrestling the Walrus* for The 154 Collective. He has toured to many village halls of the UK with Spiltmilk Dance. He has worked with Compass Live Art Festival in Leeds for over a decade as the Technical Manager. Recently Matt has rediscovered a passion for working with wood and has set up a workshop in Leeds building bespoke furniture for the homes and gardens of the people of Leeds and beyond. This is not Matt's first foray into horror...

LITTLEMIGHTY | PRODUCER

LittleMighty is an independent producer based in Leeds that works with remarkable artists to make brilliant theatre happen. Their current clients include Newcastle-based Unfolding Theatre ("Thrillingly talented people" - The Guardian). Their previous work includes Silent Uproar's *A Super Happy Story (About Feeling Super Sad)*, a Fringe First

Award winner; Testament's *Blake Remixed* and *Woke* (both created in partnership with Leeds Playhouse); and Move to Stand's *Fat Man* (Vault Festival Pick of the Year Award).

HARROGATE THEATRE | CO-PRODUCING VENUE

Harrogate Theatre is a nationally respected and critically acclaimed theatre hosting a vibrant programme of drama, dance, music and comedy in their Main House, Studio Theatre, Royal Hall and Harrogate Convention Centre. Alongside a busy schedule of visiting productions, the theatre produces its own hugely popular pantomime each year, programmes the annual Harrogate Comedy Festival and co-produces a season of REP. Together with a dedicated and vibrant education and outreach department that delivers throughout Harrogate & District, it also supports artists in making new work and is home to a number of community companies who regularly perform throughout the year.

SQUARE CHAPEL ARTS CENTRE | CO-PRODUCING VENUE

Square Chapel CIC is an arts venue in the centre of Halifax (West Yorkshire) and the beating, red brick heart of a remarkable cultural quarter for the town. Providing a unique platform for a diverse range of high-quality live performance, events and film, Square Chapel Arts Centre is a vibrant hub for culture, community and creativity. Square Chapel Trust (1988-2020) previously supported and co-commissioned new work by Adam Z Robinson, including *Upon the Stair* (2019) and *Shivers* (2017).

THE BOOK OF DARKNESS & LIGHT

The Book of Darkness & Light was created by writer Adam Z. Robinson and musician Ben Styles. Originally conceived for Light Night Leeds in 2015, the premise was simple: original, gothic tales told live to the sounds of the violin. At that first event, over 1,500 people came to see and listen to a ghost story told in the beautiful, atmospheric surroundings of Leeds's oldest church.

Afterwards, Adam and Ben went on to create a 'Ghost Stories for Christmas' show which played two sold-out performances at the Hyde Park Book Club, Leeds. In June 2016, the company received support from Arts Council England to tour their first theatrical show, *The Book of Darkness & Light*. In autumn/winter of that year, the play visited libraries, theatres and arts spaces. The show received further support from Arts Council England to play at 23 theatres for a 2017 national tour.

Shivers, the follow-up to *The Book of Darkness & Light*, was developed in association with Square Chapel Arts Centre, Harrogate Theatres and LittleMighty. It was supported by Arts Council England. The show premiered in September 2017 at Square Chapel before a run of four performances at Harrogate Theatre in January 2018. The show toured from October 2018 to March 2019, playing at more than 30 venues nationally.

In December 2019 and December 2021 the company toured Adam Z. Robinson's adaptation of *A Christmas Carol* by Charles Dickens. The production went on to have a three-week run at Baron's Court Theatre in December 2022.

Development for *Upon the Stair* began in 2019. The project was supported using public funding by Arts Council England. It was created in association with partners Square Chapel Arts Centre, Harrogate Theatres and LittleMighty. *Upon the Stair* had its world premiere at Square Chapel Arts Centre on

11 January 2020 before three performances at Salisbury Playhouse and a week-long run in Harrogate Theatre's main house.

The company are currently working on several more touring productions. Join the mailing list for updates.

www.thebookofdarknessandlight.com

FOREWORD

Note: This introduction includes plot details of the stories within the play.

The initial spark for *Upon the Stair* came in summer 2018. At that time, we were preparing to embark on a mammoth national tour of *Shivers,* the second show in The Book of Darkness & Light canon. I had a few ideas for some new tales and director/producer Dick Bonham and I were frequently discussing what the next production might look like. We had a sense that TBODAL 3 (its affectionate working title) was going to be our most ambitious project to date. As well as increasing the number of performers on stage, we wanted to make the next show accessible to more people, while further enhancing that thrilling, chilling experience we always strive to create.

The idea of integrating BSL into one of our productions had always been something that interested us. We were excited at the prospect and had many questions. In August 2018 we met, for the first time, with the brilliant Jeni Draper of fingersmiths. Jeni and her company work with Deaf and hearing actors, performing theatre in BSL and spoken English. This initial conversation was absolutely illuminating. One take-home, among many, was: work with the experts. Indeed, something I learned while working on *Upon the Stair* is if you want to make theatre for Deaf audiences you absolutely must work with Deaf artists to create the work.

At around about the same time, I began some exciting conversations with Porl Cooper (Harrogate Theatre) and Ali Ford (formerly Square Chapel Arts Centre). Both Porl and Ali have been incredible supporters of The Book of Darkness & Light, for which I'm so grateful. These conversations were really positive and securing the support of these two fantastic partners allowed us to move forward with the project with confidence.

In January 2019, armed with a few wispy ideas for stories, we got together in a rehearsal room. 'We' was Dick, Jeni, musician and composer Chloe Hayward, and actor, writer and BSL consultant EJ Raymond. We spent two days just trying things out. This was when things started to click into place for me; it's when the spark started to grow. Back in October 2018, on a few of the *Shivers* dates, we'd been lucky enough to work with BSL interpreter Lauren Lister. I saw, in Lauren's interpretation, some of the potential of how BSL might be used to bring our horror shows to life in a more physical and visual way. Working with EJ electrified this potential. As I watched them performing a version of my story 'Girl, Dancing' I realised (despite having no BSL myself at that time) just how thrilling and wholly engrossing this extra visual element was. After those incredible two days, I was so eager to get back into the rehearsal room to make the show. But there were things to do first... like write the script.

As with its predecessors, *Upon the Stair* is made up of three weird tales, brought to life through storytelling. The story I began working on first was actually the one I completed last. It would be the final and longest story of the trio. The initial inspiration came in December 2017 when I visited the Strahov Monastery in Prague. One of the more curious exhibits on display in this stunning 17th century abbey was their xylotheque. I had never seen anything quite like it; a library seemingly made of the trees it documented and catalogued. Simple to define, utterly bizarre and almost sublime to encounter. It was such a creepy-looking object and, right away, I began considering how it might be used in a ghostly tale. Even the name had a slightly mysterious M.R. James vibe about it. I made some notes and then put the idea on a shelf in the back of my mind and let it fester. Almost exactly one year later, I paid a visit to The Old Operating Theatre Museum & Herb Garret near London Bridge. Their collection of dried herbs, pharmaceutical bottles and jars, surgical apparatus and insect-related remedies (silkworm gut ligatures, concentrated maggot wash and so on), not to mention the incredibly informative talk on the history of surgical theatres, brought the xylotheque back to the fore and the all-important 'what if?' facet of the writing machine began to turn over: What if an overly ambitious scientist tried to combine his learnings in anatomy and dendrology? What if the thing he created died on the operating table but was later resurrected through occult practices? What if it took revenge on its creator, spelling their mutual doom, leaving the spectre to haunt its birthplace? And what if someone inadvertently awoke it decades later...? And so, prototypes for Dr Esther Blackwood, Godfrey Isaiah Leach and his tragic, abominable Creation were born.

Conjuring the ideas, as always, was the fun part. The writing and sculpting of 'The Xylotheque' transpired to be really challenging. I considered abandoning the tale so many times. I always over-write initially. My first drafts are huge, sprawling, over-detailed, over-researched (is that possible?), unwieldy and not at all suitable for theatre. Sometimes, once you've unpacked all of those creative boxes, it's hard to stuff the contents back in, and what you're left with is an untameable mess. With every draft, the story was becoming more complicated, not simpler as I had intended. Esther started out as a tree expert. But, try as I might, I could not get her inside Willowfield Manor long enough for the story to unfold. There wasn't a good reason for her to do the things I needed her to do for the tale to progress. I knew that the problem was huge but the solution would be simple. After bouncing the ideas off of several people, I spent a day working with Dick Bonham and in those few hours, we rewrote the entire structure of 'The Xylotheque'. Esther became an archivist on a professional engagement to recover Dr Leach's infamous library. Mr Tallent, the groundskeeper, and his faithful old collie, Bess, were sketched out, and everything now had a purpose. The truth is, though, I had reservations about the story right up until rehearsal; most likely because I felt a little bruised by the difficult writing process. Even though the story now worked, I worried that it was a little too weird and that audiences might struggle to connect with it. But, as I was delighted to discover, it turned out to be a favourite among most people I spoke to after the shows. I'm so glad I persevered and I'm grateful to Dick and the rest of the team for seeing what I initially couldn't about the story's grotesque charm.

In December 2018, I was taken to a lecture about the Krampus myth at The Pathology Museum at St Bart's Hospital in London; a Christmas present from my partner Anna (she knows me very well indeed). The evening turned out to be a hugely inspiring. First, before the lecture began, as we browsed the preserved specimens contained in the glass cabinets that made up the walls of the event space, I spotted an item with the following description: "A portion of the stomach of a horse showing numerous larvae of the bot fly." I used this unbelievably horrible, trypophobia-inducing image as a basis for the description of The Creation's face in 'The Xylotheque' ("The face, potted with holes; like honeycomb or worm-infested wood..."). The lecture itself set my mind working on another story, too. The final scene of 'The Cry of the Bubák' popped into my head as the lecturer took us through the history of Krampus, showing slides that detailed the fable's origin. 'Imagine if', I thought, 'during a lecture on folklore, you saw a horrific image of some supposedly mythical creature that you had, in fact, encountered in real life but had always rationally dismissed as nonsense'. At a later point, I spotted and read a short online article on 'the bubák' (whose origin and specifics differ across the many pieces written on it). Apparently the Czech word for the fabled 'sack man' and/or 'the bogey man', many descriptions of the bubák suggest it is a scarecrow-esque figure who can imitate the sound of a crying baby. I started to consider... to whom might that sound be most distressing? What sort of narrative would lead to such a haunting? The bubák, like the threats in most of my favourite ghost stories, hangs about in the background as a manifestation of Barraclough's guilt. The actual story, of course, is about something else entirely, something more human and more distressing than any monster. I wrote a draft of this when I was out in Cyprus leading writing workshops for school pupils. I remember the first draft just pouring out of me. It required lots of care and attention to whittle it down to what finally appeared on stage but those initial images of the tall figure hiding in the reeds at this remote spot came quickly, and I found myself unable to think of much else until I had completed a version of the story I was happy with. I really quite like it, too (if that's not too conceited a thing to say): it's neat, melancholic and, as we discovered on stage, it wallops you just at the right moments.

As for 'Mirrorman', readers of *The Book of Darkness & Light* and *Shivers* play texts will know that I have spoken previously about the 'difficult middle story'. I think the second tale in a trio like this should be both a palate-cleanser and a gear change. During the intense period redrafting 'Bubák' and 'The Xylotheque', with just a few months to go until I had to present a script to the team, an additional concern was that I simply didn't have an idea for the middle story. I didn't have a clue what it would be, how it would be structured or what would make it distinct from the other two tales. And then, one morning... it was just there, in my head. Or, the skeleton of the idea was, anyway. I revisited the first draft of 'Mirrorman' before writing this introduction. It's topped with some telltale excitable notes, written that very morning, which bullet-point the whole story: "Birthday cakes. Weird tradition: blowing out a single candle. Wishes. Covered mirrors. Dead previous occupant? Family new to the house. Sister told lies by bully brother. 'He lives in the mirror. And you let him out.'" As the ideas started to grow, I had a sense that I wanted to write something that had a fairy tale feel; a lyrical, old fashioned revenge tale where an oppressor gets their comeuppance. The first draft is remarkably close to story as performed in *Upon the Stair*. If you write, you'll know that sometimes this just happens; a story arrives fully formed and you just have to type it up. It's rare and it's precious and I wish it happened every time! During rehearsal we made the decision that my character wouldn't be present on stage at all for 'Mirrorman' and that the story would be performed entirely by Raphaella 'Raffie' Julien in BSL and VV (visual vernacular - as performing artist and consultant on this project Brian Duffy explains it: "think mime but in HD") with a voice-over by Lynsey Jones. I think it was one of the best calls we made in the entire production;

that was what made 'Mirrorman' stand out and what made it worthy of the all-important middle spot.

In July 2019, we were lucky enough to receive support from Arts Council England to make and perform *Upon the Stair*. Finding out that our application had been successful was a huge moment. Afterwards, things seemed to happen very quickly. Through Jeni Draper, we met our BSL consultant - the inimitable Brian Duffy; Raffie absolutely stormed her audition and we knew, instantly, she'd be the perfect fit for the role of The Shade (another reluctant storyteller in the book's thrall); Chloe Hayward and I met up to discuss and try out some of the music for the production... and so the foundations were laid. We then assembled the rest of the team: Emma Williams (Set and Costume Designer), Tim Skelly (Lighting Designer), Matt Sykes-Hooban (Technical Stage Manager), Guy Connelly (Sound Designer), Adam Bassett (BSL Consultant) and, so suddenly, it seemed, we were in the rehearsal room.

I hadn't worked with Deaf artists before *Upon the Stair* but I embraced the opportunity. The translation process from written English into BSL and VV was intensive and an incredible thing to be a part of. Working with Duffy, Jeni, and later Adam Bassett, Raffie began to bring the tales off the page and into performance. I remember, early in the first week, leaving the room to go and memorise some lines so that we could bring everything together. When I returned, I saw the tail-end of a scene that Duffy and Raffie had been working on. It was the moment in *Bubák* when Barraclough is being beckoned to his demise by the creature in the reeds. It stopped me in my tracks. It was like watching a movie, only performed entirely by a single person. Not only did I understand and follow every beat of the performance, I was totally riveted, chilled and terrified by what I was seeing. It was then, I think, that I realised our goal was not just to make a show that was accessible; it was to try to create something equally thrilling for every single person in the audience.

I want to do a shout out here to our incredible team of interpreters. Headed up by the brilliant Julie Thompson, Alun Jones, Stephanie Raper, Sarah Cox, Sarah Sheen, Jen Phoenix, Dave Wycherley, Claire Dodds and Rebekah Mills were all so wonderful to work with. We had two interpreters present at every rehearsal day and it was so great to learn from them as we made the show.

Developing moments such as the cot scene in 'Bubák', the final scare in 'Mirrorman', and the cabinet scene in 'The Xylotheque' marked pivotal landmarks in the company's creative development, and they're memories I treasure. I remember a day when Raffie and I were discussing how The Creation in the final story might move. To demonstrate her ideas, Raffie stood up and started buckling and popping and staggering and moving her body in the most brilliantly horrific way: "Something like that?" If you saw the show, you'll surely remember that encounter and recognise what a talent Raffie is for making the written material live in such haunting, vivid and magnificent ways.

The rehearsal process was challenging for everyone in the team. Our ambition almost became our ultimate adversary. So, it's hard to describe my feelings during tech week at Square Chapel Arts Centre in January 2020 as everything started to come together. Seeing Emma Williams' set for the first time, lit by Tim Skelly's incredible lighting design, hearing Guy Connolly's eerie and terrifying sound design in tandem with Chloe's compositions, and witnessing a whole team of people dedicated to making my ghost stories come to life was a sensation I'll never forget: a combination of appreciation, gratitude, excitement... and terror. Despite the challenges, time constraints and bumps in the road, everything lined up. That's a testament to the outstanding team I had the privilege of working with on this project. We did our tech run, our dress rehearsal and we performed *Upon the Stair* for the first time on Saturday 11 January 2020 at Square Chapel Arts Centre, Halifax (my home town). I don't remember that show, I was too fizzy with adrenaline, but I remember the feeling of elation afterwards when the applause came and that incredible feeling of "we did it" started to settle in. We received some of the best comments we've ever had for *Upon the Stair*, from Deaf and hearing audiences alike. I've never been prouder of anything I've worked on.

After Square Chapel, we moved on to Salisbury Playhouse where we really started to hone the show and make it our own. By the end of those performances we were ready for our week-long run at Harrogate Theatre. We performed across a whole week in the beautiful main house. Harrogate Theatre have been so generous in their support of my work for years, and performing on their main stage has been something of a professional ambition for a long time. I made sure to stop and take stock, during that incredible week; to be in the moment and appreciate what was happening. I'd often go onto the stage, a couple of hours before that night's show, and reflect on where things had started for this project and where they were now. It was an extraordinary week and I was so proud to be able to share the stage with Chloe and

Raffie as we did what would transpire to be the final performances of *Upon the Stair*. Our last show (for now, at least!) was on Saturday 29 February 2020.

I'm so thrilled that you hold in your hands another way for us to send this play out into the world. I sincerely hope that you'll one day have a chance to see it performed live, as it was intended to be. I have a feeling, where this play is concerned, there is unfinished business. For now, though, I really hope you enjoy reading *Upon the Stair*.

Adam Z. Robinson

June 2022

THANK YOU AND ACKNOWLEDGEMENTS

I'd like to say a huge thank you to: my incredible colleagues on this project: Dick Bonham, Raffie Julien, Chloe Hayward, Matt Sykes-Hooban, Emma Williams, Tim Skelly, Guy Connelly, Jeni Draper, Adam Bassett, Brian Duffy, our wonderful team of BSL interpreters: Julie Thompson, Alun Jones, Steph Raper, Sarah Cox, Sarah Sheen, Jen Phoenix, Dave Wycherley, Claire Dodds and Rebekah Mills. I learned so much from every single person working on this show. Our wonderful friends at Harrogate Theatre and Square Chapel Arts Centre, past a present, who were instrumental in making the show happen (especially Linzi, Al, Rachel, Tori, Kerry, Michaela, Mo, Sam, Martin, Dave, Sofia, Alec, David, Adam, and a special thanks to Dee our venue technician for the tech week and premiere performances). An extra special thanks to Porl Cooper and to Ali Ford for all of their support, friendship and belief in The Book of Darkness & Light – I appreciate every single opportunity you've given me. Our friends at Interplay Theatre for their support and space during rehearsal. Our friends at Slung Low (past and present), Alan, Joanna, Sally, Matt and James for letting us rehearse in your brilliant space. EJ Raymond for being such an important part of the early-stage R&D process. Jimmy Ragg for building our amazing set. Our assistant scene painter Rhiannon Hodgson for all of her hard work during production. Barnaby Aldrick for our outstanding photography. Wayne Gamble for our awesome marketing materials. James Hodges at Infinite Media for our trailer. Wayne Sables for capturing the live performance on film. Nick Goddard for his expertise on trees and botany, and Kew Gardens for help and information during the writing period of 'The Xylotheque'. Martin Wiseman for his help with the

Latin terms. Sarah Cockburn for her brilliant admin support. Dr Vivien Sabel for her incredible support and championing of the project. Barrie Long for his input during the early stages of production – his feedback was invaluable and gave us so much confidence in the show. Deaf Café, Harrogate, for their feedback on 'Mirrorman' ahead of the first performances. Mike Muncer at the Evolution of Horror podcast (highly recommend to all horror fans) for his ongoing support of our work. Rhianna Dhillon for running lines with me on the lead up to final rehearsals. Becky Darke, our fantastic proofreader. Nick Coupe and Andy Craven-Griffiths for being early readers and sounding boards for the tales. My wonderful supporters on Patreon (join me for audio productions and workshops: www.patreon.com/adamzrobinson) and the fantastic community that came together online during the Covid-19 pandemic (www.facebook.com/groups/AZRevents). All of our supporters across Facebook, Twitter and Instagram. Elliot Robinson and our publishers Playdead Press. Our wonderful producers, LittleMighty. Hannah Bentley and Arts Council England for supporting the project and tour. Every single person who came along to see the play in 2020. My secondary school English teacher, Carol Stoker, to whom this book is dedicated, for igniting that initial spark and interest in writing at such a crucial stage in my life.

And extra special thanks to Anna Wiseman for everything, always.

A NOTE ON PERFORMANCE

In the original production of *Upon the Stair*, the characters of The Storyteller and The Shade told the stories in tandem, in their own ways. The Storyteller (Adam Z. Robinson) used spoken English and The Shade (Raphaella Julien) used BSL and VV (visual vernacular). We worked with Deaf artists and expert consultants to translate the script to this end. We also took longer, more descriptive passages from the stories and presented them using VV, movement and physical performance in lieu of the words as written. The Storyteller and The Shade maintained a single, unique persona for each story - i.e. the narrator of each tale, occasionally creating moments of dialogue between two characters. There are, however, several other character voices throughout the tales that can be presented as audio recordings, or a larger ensemble may be used to bring the stories to life. Do whatever works best for your production and split up The Storyteller's and The Shade's lines as you wish.

Adam Z. Robinson

Yesterday, upon the stair,
I met a man who wasn't there!
He wasn't there again today,
Oh how I wish he'd go away!

- 'Antigonish', William Hughes Mearns

CHARACTERS

On stage:
THE STORYTELLER
THE SHADE
THE MUSICIAN

In the tales:
SIR SIMON WALPOLE
ROBERT BARRACLOUGH
ALBERT RUDGE
TIPPI
BROTHER
MOTHER
ESTHER BLACKWOOD
VAUGHAN TALLENT
BESS (AN OLD COLLIE)
GODFREY ISAIAH LEACH
THE CREATION

This text is based on the script used in rehearsals and so may differ slightly from the play as performed.

PROLOGUE

Set: Wood-panelled walls, broken windows, buckling book shelves, library steps, a covered mirror, a gramophone on a stand with vinyl records scattered beneath.

Darkness. Howling wind. Tormented voices. Creak of trees. Breaking of glass.

The sounds rise and crescendo. Then, cut to silence.

Low light up on...

THE SHADE. She's holding The Book of Darkness & Light. She regards it fearfully. She curses it; wishes herself free of its hold over her.

THE STORYTELLER and THE MUSICIAN enter.

THE STORYTELLER approaches THE SHADE. She tries to pass the book on. Reluctantly, he takes it. They pass it back and forth throughout.

THE STORYTELLER, THE SHADE and THE MUSICIAN tell the stories in tandem, each in their own way.

STORYTELLER/SHADE:

> This book is our burden. And we are its captives.
>
> It is a tome of unquiet tales, a litany of horrors. These pages absorb humanity's darkest stories and – sometimes – the souls of the all-too-curious.

THE STORYTELLER looks at THE SHADE. She seems to cower and cringe with regret.

Our sentence compels us from one place to the next; to seek out those with gruesome hearts and a will to witness the terrors within this Book of Darkness & Light.

Tonight, the book has brought us here. To [town/city], as wicked and fearful a place as we have ever frequented. (*Looking at the audience*) Yes, a wretched gathering, indeed.

Three tales will be shared.

But before we begin, a warning to the curious: From the moment the first page is turned, you, all, enter into a pact with the book. Its terms are not known to us. We cannot say what you might take away with you... nor what you will leave behind. By remaining here, you enter into this arrangement of your own free will.

Or... flee. Go. Turn your back on this night and begin tomorrow free.

THE STORYTELLER gestures towards the exits. Waits for people to leave. When they don't...

Then you are beyond redemption.

And so, to the tales...

THE STORYTELLER and THE SHADE wrench open the pages. THE MUSICIAN plays a strained chord and moves into...

MUSIC: *Upon the Stair* **main theme**

THE CRY OF THE BUBÁK

1.

MUSIC: Transition/segue

STORYTELLER/SHADE:

> Today, on the north bank of the mighty river Vltava, some seventy miles south of Prague, there stands the derelict shell of a great, crescent-shaped building. It was, once, a world-renowned health facility. In its heyday the institution was known affectionately, by patients and practitioners alike, as 'The Horseshoe'. It is the site of our first tale.
>
> The story is taken from a sworn account by Sir Simon Walpole (of whose writings on Biblical apocrypha you may well be familiar). The account details Sir Simon's own brief stay at The Horseshoe, which resulted in a most singular reunion.

THE STORYTELLER and THE SHADE take on the role of WALPOLE.

2.

MUSIC: Bubák theme

WALPOLE: I have often been asked the question "Do you believe in ghosts?"

31

Before the circumstances that I am about to relate, I would have invariably and emphatically answered: "no".

Ever since those events, however, I continue to find that I am not so resigned on the position.

There was, I have always felt, something significant about my reunion with Robert Barraclough; some preordained reason why I was present to 'bear witness'. I have never been able to make sense of what took place, out there in the Czech countryside. But now, as a man of seventy-five and prompted by a recent, chilling sequel, I finally commit this horrible story to paper.

3.

WALPOLE: Eight months before the events that came to pass, I lost my dear sister, Lucy, to a violent strain of influenza. The loss hit me hard. Neither one of us was married and our parents were long since in the grave. So, each of us was all the other had.

I became a mere husk; a broken man who was, frankly, waiting eagerly for the end.

It was my dear friend, Albert Rudge, who pulled me out of this depressive mire. We had been course-mates at Cambridge - both of us there on scholarships – and had remained very close. It was on Alby's insistence that I traveled to

Zilkova and registered myself as a patient at 'The Horseshoe' Health Facility. Alby himself had been a physician there, briefly, after the war, and spoke in the highest possible terms of its programme of innovative treatments.

In truth, I harboured little hope of recovering my former *joie de vivre* or, in fact, any solace whatsoever. And so it was, to my very great surprise, that the methods employed began to have an impact on my state of mind more or less immediately. In short, as the weeks went by, I began to feel better. And, though my grief was still raw, I was able to focus my attention on a hopeful future.

All of this, I must stress, is mere detail to provide an adequate prologue for what is to follow.

4.

Walpole's room

WALPOLE: It was, I distinctly remember, a Wednesday. I had been at The Horseshoe for twenty days and nights.

I'd had my weekly assessment with Dr. Linsenmaier and had retired for my customary midday nap. The room was stuffy, and so I opened the window. I was enchanted for a moment by the splendid view: the great river's progress, the tall, swaying reeds lining the banks in thick rows, the small jetty onto which I had stepped just three weeks before. And, there *was* the ferry, just departing. And yes, emerging through the front gate was our latest resident...

That the fellow was Robert Barraclough, I was in no doubt. I recognised him upon the instant. And, despite not having seen him in over a decade, I had a familiar sensation, not unlike nervous excitement.

Barraclough had been an acquaintance – perhaps even something of a hero of mine – at Cambridge.

In those days, he was rather the life and soul of the party; bombastic and charismatic with a devil-may-care spirit. He had a tendency to indulge in many a fleeting friendship and, only in hindsight, have I reflected that he treated most of us quite as if we were currency. Once spent up, he would move on to some shinier treasure. Nevertheless, his company was always thrilling and greatly sought after. It is fair to say that Barraclough made a lingering impression on me.

And here he was, now, walking towards The Horseshoe.

What strange fortune. *How nice it would be* – I thought – *to catch up*. And yet, as I watched him struggle through the gates, an unnameable sense of gloom began to descend...

There was something disquieting about his movements – though nothing that could be put down to age or ailment. It was something more *essential*. The Barraclough I had known would stride through campus, shoulders back, smile radiating. This fellow slouched dreadfully and shuffled more than walked, up the shale path.

He paused for a moment, put down his bulging suitcases, produced a hip flask and took a surreptitious nip. Then a second.

WALPOLE turns around sharply, to indicate BARRACLOUGH's movement.

Something had evidently startled him. He was now staring out towards the river.

He took bird-like half-steps; first this way and then that, bobbing his head, as if trying to catch sight of something obscured in the reeds. I, myself, could see nothing.

But in this manner he was thus engaged for several minutes. Finally, either satisfied or frustrated in his vigil, Barraclough collected his belongings from the shingle and turned towards the facility once more...

And in doing so, he looked directly at my window.

MUSIC: Slow, melancholy chords

There was a moment's pause. Then, without any evidence of surprise or shock at seeing a familiar face in this strange setting, he simply raised his hand, in a limp sort of wave.

Momentarily, he began trudging towards the entrance again.

MUSIC: *Bubák theme variation*

I cast a final glance towards the river. And there I fancied I *did* see... *something*. In the reeds. A figure, perhaps. Certainly, there was the vaguest suggestion of dark clothing, retreating towards the water.

Barraclough had, by now, moved out of sight.

"Perhaps I should go and welcome him," I thought.

"No, no. I'll see him at dinner. Best let the fellow settle in..."

MUSIC stops

5.

Dining room

WALPOLE: I did not, in fact, see Barraclough again until the following evening.

I was dining alone at my usual table, watching the sun set on the southern basin of the river when I gradually became aware of a presence at my side. It was Barraclough; gentle and quiet as a shadow.

"Barraclough!" I said. "How the hell are you! I knew it was you! Have you eaten? Food's not exactly *haute cuisine* but it's passable. Grab a plate, old boy, let's catch up!"

"I won't," he said. "Walpole, isn't it? Thanks all the same."

He looked entirely washed out. Perhaps his treatments were more rigorous than my own. That creeping sense of gloom threatened a return...

"My word," I said. "It's been, what... fifteen years?"

Barraclough feigned a smile. "And how remote we are from the hopeful young men we were."

He was staring out of the window.

"Uh... quite! Are you settling in alright?" I asked.

"They've given me a family room. With a... with a cot and what have you. I've asked them to move me."

"Those family suites are the biggest on offer!" I said. "I should keep mum!"

Barraclough merely repeated himself: "Yes. I've asked to be moved."

We chatted shallowly. I told him about my dear sister's passing. He was rather aloof about his own reasons for being at The Horseshoe – something about *wanting to get away*.

Every now and then, I saw the sheerest glimmer of the man I'd once known; a gossamer phantom of that former *bon viveur*. But it did not last nor linger.

"Well," I said, standing to depart for my final treatment of the day. "I hope there'll be more opportunities to reminisce now we're both *inmates*, eh?"

WALPOLE turns to leave.

MUSIC: Shriek

I felt a sudden pain in my forearm. Barraclough had grabbed me; five, long, unkempt nails digging into my skin.

"I say – you're hurting, there…"

"Sshh!" His eyes bulged in his head. "Can you hear it?"

"What?"

"Ssshh! Listen…"

He pointed towards the river bank. I strained to hear what had provoked such a violent reaction…

FX: Something grows, faintly. Then…

FX: LOUD, SUDDEN, a service trolley comes clattering by

The clatter of the dining trolley pierced the tension and Barraclough loosed his grip of my arm.

"I'm *afraid*," I said. "I didn't hear anything."

"No. No, of course not."

"Yes, well. Do take care of yourself, old boy. I'll see you tomorrow, perhaps?"

He did not respond.

As I left him there, I heard him mutter something to himself. It was just too indistinct for me to be certain but it sounded rather like: "Won't be long, now."

MUSIC: Bubák theme

6.

The grounds

WALPOLE: Next morning, before breakfast, I went on one of my walks around the grounds. It was overcast but bright. The sky had turned a sugary-brown by the time I'd completed my usual circuit. It was early and I didn't see a soul... until I neared the river bank.

MUSIC: Bubák theme variation

FX: The reeds

Throughout my stay, we'd been given various admonitions about straying aimlessly into the reeds (no doubt, previous patients had fallen foul of the sudden drop into the river whilst on their own perambulations). I'd been obedient to these warnings but, demonstrably, others were not so prudent... for somebody was stalking about in the tall plants. They were mostly obscured but I had an impression of an incredibly thin personage with flapping clothing. Whomever it was, was stooping and hunched and moving erratically at quite a pace.

I was about to call out a warning but, in the very next moment, whoever had been there appeared to vanish from sight. I had a momentary fear that they had fallen into the river. But it was a quiet morning and there was no such sound to confirm my suspicion.

The reeds were giving off an offensive smell. Something fetid, almost animal-like. It was overwhelming and I was compelled to return to the comforts of indoors, where I could report the matter.

FX: Sinister tone, tension rises

I turned... and almost barged headlong into a man standing behind me. It was Barraclough. He was staring past me towards the reeds. An expectant, anxious look was on his face; as though he were intently listening for something.

"Barraclough? BARRACLOUGH?"

He looked me dead in the eyes, tears swimming in his own.

"I should have done right by them!" he said. "But now it's too late. Don't you see? It's too late."

I felt it would have been wrong of me to agitate him further with interrogation, and so I put a kindly arm around him and led him inside.

7.

MUSIC: Light, underpinning the dialogue

WALPOLE: It was several days before I had another encounter with Barraclough. I would occasionally spot him, sitting in the day room or loitering in the library. Sometimes, I'd spy him from my bedroom window, shuffling around the grounds. On these latter occasions, he seemed to return to his preoccupation with the river bank; staring as if in anticipation of something that was coming.

He was always alone.

MUSIC stops

8.

Lounge

WALPOLE: Everything came to a head about two weeks after Barraclough arrived at The Horseshoe.

I was on my way to speak to Dr. Linsenmaier about my own imminent departure, when I spotted Barraclough slumped in an easy chair, brazenly swigging from his hip flask.

"Better not let anyone see you with your medicine there, old man."

FX: Low, unnerving tone

Barraclough's head snapped up. His complexion was bloodless; the colour of chalk.

"Whatever is the matter?" I asked, taking a seat opposite.

He shook his head and tried for a smile. "Nothing. Nothing to be done."

"Nonsense!" I said. "It's plain to me you've had some sort of shock…"

His eyes were locked upon his flask.

"Well, in actual fact, I have. But I wonder if I ought to tell you, in all honesty… That room. I shan't stay in it another night. I'll sleep down here if I have to…"

"Take a deep breath," I said. "There's a good fellow. Now, tell me what's happened."

Barraclough inhaled deeply, took another swallow from his flask. And this is what he told me…

MUSIC: Sinister and erratic

"You'll remember, won't you, that they've put me in a family room? Well, the fact is, I haven't been sleeping well. Last night, there was a bright moon – perhaps you saw – and, like a damned fool, I'd forgotten to pull my drapes and the light woke me. I got up to close them... and I glanced over at that wretched cot in the corner. Only I wish to God that I hadn't. There was *bedding* in it, Walpole. Sheets with animals on... else, shapes. The sort you get in nurseries."

I tried to look reassuring and was about to ask *what was so terrible about that?* Barraclough intercepted my question.

FX: *Low tones increase tension*

"No, no, don't you see? *It wasn't there before. And it's not there now.* And there's more... the sheets, were covering something. Something small. And it was moving. Gently, up and down like... breathing. And then... dear God... It *turned over.* Slowly. Towards me. It did not seem human to me. But it had human hands. *Tiny*, hands with thin fingers that reached out and gripped the bars of the cot. It started to pull itself up to standing; it was a small thing, a *young* thing, and, Walpole, it was *crying.* But the sound wasn't coming from it. What I mean to say is that I could see its *mouth was going,* as *though* it were crying. But the *sound* was coming from *out there.* Outside. From down by the river. I've heard it before. And then... it started to climb

43

out of the cot... Well I *ran*, Walpole! I ran! One of the orderlies found me and marched me back to the room, despite my protests. And when we got there... The cot was empty. No bedding. Nothing."

MUSIC stops

Barraclough glanced about us, half-crazed, and another thought seemed to arrest him suddenly.

"Walpole, answer me this... there's plenty of wildlife down on those river banks - that's right, isn't it? But it's not *farmland*, is it? And nothing is *grown* down there? Only the reeds? So there'd be no need, would there... for there to be a scarecrow? No? Anyway. It's gone now. Oh, it's my fault. My fault. Won't be long now. Soon, there'll be no resisting."

He broke down, wracked with a fresh wave of sobs.

Barraclough was moved to a different room that same day.

9.

Telephone room

MUSIC: Sombre, melancholy

FX: Light thunderstorm outside, whipping winds

WALPOLE: The following evening, I received a telephone call from Alby – my old university chum who'd recommended The Horseshoe to me in the first place. He was calling to check on my progress, and to ask when I might be returning home etc. As was the way with us, our conversations quickly turned towards the many tales of our shared history... and, soon, to my recent strange encounter.

"Speaking of blasts from the past, you'll never guess who's recently become a resident here..."

The line went quiet.

"It wouldn't be... Robert Barraclough?"

"Well... yes, exactly. How on earth did you guess that?"

"I recommended the place to him. I ran into him at Charing Cross last November. Took him for a brandy at my club, poor devil. He was in quite a state! Not a bit like I remembered... Told me he'd had some bitter disagreement with his father and the two were no longer in communication. You remember his father, I suppose? Generous donor to the college. But quite a tyrant towards Barraclough. The poor fellow had no say in his own future. Immediately after Cambridge he was established as a junior and made to work up the ranks. And work he did. For well over a decade. Only, when I saw him in November, he told me he'd been let go. Wasn't even offered a severance. Told me he was considering going away. Asked me about my time in Zilkova. I never thought for a second he'd go out there! He rambled a lot. Kept saying things like, '*It's going to catch up with me, anyhow.*' Wouldn't say what he meant. But I have an idea... You know about his young woman and the child, I assume? Dreadful business. Barraclough was involved with a woman in Halifax. She worked at one of the factories. It was love, so everybody said. She fell pregnant. Barraclough wanted to do the right thing. But his father forbade the union. Threatened to cut him off entirely. So... Barraclough abandoned her. That poor woman. She was thrown out by her family. Had the baby alone. A boy. Soon afterwards, she left the poor little mite with the nuns at St Augustine's Priory. And then she threw herself off North Bridge. The baby died of consumption. Last spring. Just a year old, he was. Since then, I gather, Barraclough has been rather a different man. Stood up to his father. But rather too late. As I say: dreadful business."

A cold realisation hits WALPOLE.

10.

Walpole's room

MUSIC: *Mournful*

WALPOLE: There is a final incident which I must relate to bring this sorry tale to a close.

46

It happened very early on the morning I was due to leave the facility. I had not seen Barraclough in over a week. In truth, I had been avoiding him.

MUSIC stops

FX: *A low, ominous tone*

I'd fallen asleep in my chair by the window, book in lap. When I woke, dawn was just threatening to break on a particularly misty morning.

The curve of the building allowed me to observe that, of the dozens of windows visible, only one was lit up. And, at that window stood a figure, half in silhouette. It was Barraclough. He was staring, unflinchingly, out towards the water.

FX: *Strange, unsettling*

He appeared to be sobbing. With his hands, he was gesturing oddly – a strange alternation between waving gayly and warding off some approaching tormentor. His gaze was fixed upon the riverbank.

I looked towards the water... And saw *something* protruding from the reeds. The morning mist hindered my view some but I could have sworn that it was nothing less than a long, thin arm, reaching from under a tatty garment; the hand, moving, as if to beckon.

I had, in my trunk, a pair of field glasses and I went to retrieve them. At length I returned to the window. But a scan of the reeds, this time, discovered nothing at all. *I must have been mistaken*, I thought.

I looked again at Barraclough's window.

FX: Strange, unsettling, increases, becomes unbearably tense

He was gone. But a moment or two later, I saw him emerge from The Horseshoe by the front entrance.

He moved, so very queerly, across the shale and through the gate. It was as though - how can I put this? As though he were being dragged against his will.

I hammered on the window.

"Barraclough!"

His head turned and he saw me. His face was a mask of all-consuming fear and, though I could not hear, I knew from that desperate expression that he was screaming for his life.

His pace quickened. And then, as he neared the riverbank, I saw some unimaginable, inhuman shape step forwards, part the reeds with two horribly thin arms and envelope Barraclough, as if in some terrible embrace. How can I describe the face? That awful body? Those hellish rags?

It dragged my old friend into the darkness of the reeds as though he were nothing more than a rolled-up carpet.

FX: Crescendos

I fled my room and raised the alarm. I had the presence of mind not to give the full details of what I had seen; I knew I would not be believed. Nor did I fully understand it myself.

A search party was mounted. Despite my protestations, I was obliged to wait indoors. The initial search, on account of the fog, which had swelled and risen dramatically, was fruitless.

11.

Linsenmaier's office

MUSIC: Sparse, pizzicato

WALPOLE: I spent the morning sitting with Dr Linsenmaier. The doctor insisted that Barraclough had most likely stepped out for some morning air. He sent me off for breakfast after which time, he assured me, Barraclough would have returned and the whole matter would seem rather silly and distant.

FX: The riverbank

Barraclough's body was found just before noon.

The caretaker was conducting his errands around the jetty. The remains were half submerged in the river.

MUSIC: Ominous notes and chords, slow

I saw the caretaker as he awaited the arrival of the coroner. He was holding a glass of water with trembling hands and talking (in the native language) to one of the nurses, who was trying, in vain, to pacify him.

I understood hardly anything of the conversation but there was a phrase which he repeated several times: '*neměl kůži; neměl maso*'. I noted it down – a decision that I'd come to regret deeply.

'*Neměl kůži; neměl maso.*'

'He had no skin. He had no flesh.'

The coroner's report suggested that Barraclough had been mauled to death by some wild animal.

MUSIC stops

12.

Lecture hall

WALPOLE: That really is the end of the story, save for this recent sequel which happened just three weeks ago; some thirty five years after the events at The Horseshoe. You may take it how you please.

I was in attendance at a lecture – part of a Christmas series - at the University of Geneva. The lecturer was an expert in folklore studies. Though the content was interesting, the professor's soporific tone and the mug of mulled wine I'd swallowed were lulling me towards unconsciousness there in my seat.

But then, a new slide flashed up and banished any possibility of sleep then and for many weeks to follow. Indeed, I have not slept soundly since.

FX: Sinister, threatening

What the image showed was a charcoal impression of a beastly-thin figure wrapped in tattered clothes. Its face was obscured. It was impossibly real in the rendering. Quite as if the thing might step down from the slide, into the auditorium. I automatically reached into my breast pocket for my notepad and pencil and wrote down the caption as accurately as I could:

'Pictured is The Bubák: a most malevolent figure from European folklore, whose origins are disputed. In some depictions, the creature haunts riverbanks and is said to resemble a half-human scarecrow. It lures those whose souls weigh heavy with guilt and shame by imitating the sound of a crying infant. It is believed to weave its terrible rags from the skins of those whose souls it has stolen'.

MUSIC: Bubák theme variation

THE SHADE becomes overtaken by the spirit of The Bubák; violently tearing, thrashing and gnawing at an unseen victim. THE STORYTELLER sees this and approaches. He carefully but firmly releases her from the possession.

ACT 2

MIRRORMAN

1.

MUSIC: Transition/segue

STORYTELLER/SHADE:

> Folklore and superstition have far greater influence over us than we might care to admit.
>
> There are those of us who raise a salute on sight of a magpie. Others who cast spilled salt over their left shoulder and desperately avoid the number 13. Foolish remnants of childhood, perhaps. And, yet, we dare not risk the transgression.
>
> We may believe ourselves to be rational beings; people of reason.
>
> But the things we believe about ourselves are not always the truth. And we cling, dearly, to our rituals.
>
> This is a story about such a ritual.
>
> It comes from the transcript of a home recording; a vinyl record, discovered among the last earthly possessions of one Ms. Tippi Stoker.

THE STORYTELLER exits, into the shadows.

2.

MUSIC: Mirrorman theme

Tippi's house

A large, covered mirror upstage, centre

THE SHADE takes on the role of TIPPI.

TIPPI: Every family has traditions that are particular to them; private games and ways of bonding that would seem peculiar to outsiders.

Ours involved birthday candles. And wishes.

MUSIC: *Mirrorman theme*

Whatever age my brother or I turned, our cake would always host a solitary candle. We would sit in the dark, strike a match and light it.

We would make a wish, before blowing out the flame.

Then.

We'd strike another match and illuminate the candle once more.

This way – Mother always said – we got a wish for every year we'd been alive.

"The older we get, the more we need wishes!" she'd say. "Wishes are very powerful things, Tippi."

3.

TIPPI: On my eleventh birthday, my brother stole my birthday wishes. And all of the wishes for every birthday I would ever have.

Let me explain...

MUSIC: Slow chords

He was a cruel brother. From the moment I was born, he didn't like me. He would call me ugly. And weird. He would say that I was fat. And disgusting. He'd say that, looking as I did, nobody would ever love me. I tried not to care. After all, I didn't *want* anybody to love me - I loved myself. But, with each barbed word he spat, I loved myself less and less and believed my brother more and more...

*

When I was ten years old, Mother moved us to a ramshackle old house on the edge of town.

The house was big and cold and bleak and greasy and grim. Every stick of furniture was enveloped in decades of cobwebs and dust.

But, it had come cheap.

Because a man had died there.

MUSIC: Melodic, menacing, pizzicato

My brother told me the story. The man was a carpenter and, one dark day in autumn, while constructing a wooden chest for a rich woman, he was careless. He slipped, tripped and fell. Into the trunk. The large, heavy lid came down on top of him and he was trapped; locked inside a deep wooden chest that could only be unlocked from the outside.

MUSIC: *Thudding*

His screams could not be heard through the layers of dense timber and thick lining.

MUSIC: *Melodic, menacing*

Some said that it wasn't an accident. That he and the rich woman had quarrelled over money and she had pushed him inside and closed the lid. No-one ever really knew the truth.

The man wasted away to nothing; there inside a box of his own making.

A wasted-away man in the attic.

And now, we had to live in his house.

MUSIC stops

4.

The attic

TIPPI: The day we arrived at our new house, my brother took me into the attic.

MUSIC: *Strange, queasy*

There was a trunk, tucked away in the corner. The lid was open.

"That's where he died," said my brother.

My brother often told lies. But there was the box. I could see it with my own eyes.

He grabbed me and dragged me towards it.

"In you go, disgusting girl. Where nobody will ever have to look at you again!"

MUSIC: *Pace increases*

I screamed for Mother. But Mother could not climb the steps to the attic because her knees were bad.

I bit my brother's hand, hard, and ran.

I tumbled down the stairs and landed in a heap.

MUSIC: *Descends with tumble*

My brother laughed so hard it brought on a coughing fit.

5.

The hallway

MUSIC: *Mirrorman theme*

TIPPI: There were dozens of mirrors in the new house. When we first came to live there, each one was draped with a thick, black cloth. I loved mirrors.

I was fascinated by them. It was sad that they should all be covered up like that.

I did not ask Mother about the drapes. She was not fond of questions.

Dining room

Instead, I crept into the dining room when everybody else was busy. On the wall of this room was the greatest mirror in the whole house. I stole a look underneath the drape.

The frame was gorgeous. It was decorative and stained black. The edges of the glass were mottled with dark blossoms; like little lily pads on a moonlit lake. The mirror was a marvel to me. I wondered if the dead carpenter had made it.

FX: *Strange, tense tones*

I peeled the cover back further...

(*Sudden*) "TIPPI!" said my brother, who had snuck up beside me.

MUSIC: *Brother theme. Low, staccato*

"Don't! You'll disturb the Mirrorman!"

"Who? What do you mean?" I asked. "Why are the mirrors covered up?"

"You're so stupid," he told me. "Stupid, ugly girl. When somebody dies, you have to cover all the mirrors and open the front door of the house.

If you don't, their soul is sucked into the mirrors and gets trapped there. That's what happened to the Mirrorman."

"But who *is* the Mirrorman?" I asked.

"He's the carpenter who died in our attic. Nobody covered the mirrors until long after his soul had left his body. So it has been taken in. Now, he's the Mirrorman and his soul has turned... bad. That's why the covers are there now. To protect us. Because if you look in the mirror and you see the Mirrorman... he will reach out with his wasted, rotting hands and drag you back inside with him. Forever."

"He can't... come out, can he?" I asked.

My brother smiled his most wicked, wolfish smile.

"Yes. He can. But only once a year. On his deathday. But *we* don't know when that is. Could be any day. So you must never, ever look in the mirror."

And off he sloped, into the shadows of the house. Leaving me to stare at the black-draped frame.

MUSIC: *Mirror theme*

When Mother began uncovering the mirrors, I screamed the house down.

She told me I was a stupid girl. Fancy being afraid of my own reflection!

59

I was sent to bed, slapped, without supper.

MUSIC stops

6.

Tippi's room

MUSIC: Mirror theme

TIPPI: In my bedroom there was an enormous mirror. This one, I kept covered up. I used a black tapestry that I'd found in one of Mother's drawers.

But, I'd wake up most mornings to find the tapestry on the floor. My brother swore his innocence. And Mother never came into my room.

I'd close my eyes and re-cover it, careful not to catch my reflection staring back. Careful not to spy the Mirrorman.

FX: Sinister, menacing tones

At night, I'd lie, wide awake, and stare at the covered mirror.

Some nights, I saw the tapestry move.

MUSIC: Unnerving, threatening

I saw it grow, as if there were a hand underneath it.

A horrible wasted hand with long, rotten nails.

And sometimes, I saw the shape of the Mirrorman's face.

The black tapestry covering his bony features; his eye sockets.

His dead, wasted head.

I'd scream and cry. But nobody ever came.

Sometimes I thought I saw him in the windows; for they, at night, were mirrors too.

When I paced the floors in the small hours, wide awake with terror, I would sneak past the mirrors in the hallways and sometimes I was sure that I felt a hand try to grab at me. I saw him at the edges of my vision. I so wanted to look... but I never did.

MUSIC stops

7.

Dining room

MUSIC: Mirrorman variation

TIPPI: My first birthday in that house was my eleventh over all.

Mother had gone out of town to visit our aunt, who was wealthy and sick.

She left my brother in charge. She left a small cake. She left a candle. She left eleven matches.

We sat in the dining room with the lights low. I always sat with my back to the great mirror.

My brother was being especially nice to me. *Because it's my birthday,* I thought.

Mother had left me a card:

Tippi. Happy birthday. Use your wishes wisely. Remember, wishes are powerful things.

'Ready to turn out the lights?' my brother asked me.

I nodded, delighting at the idea of eleven wishes – the most I'd ever had!

'Oh, I almost forgot...' he said, and handed me another envelope.

MUSIC: *Ominous melody, pizzicato*

I opened it.

It was a page torn from a newspaper. A story about a man who had died; had wasted away in an attic. A carpenter who had become trapped inside a box of his own making that could only be unlocked from the outside.

"Look at the date," my brother said.

MUSIC: *Low, slow*

The man had died on the 24th of October. My birthday.

"Today is his deathday! You'd better use your wishes to keep him in the mirror!"

My brother turned out the light.

I lit my first match.

(*Fearfully*) "I wish the Mirrorman would stay in the mirror!" I said. I blew out the candle.

I lit it a second time, a third, a fourth.

"I wish the Mirrorman would stay in the mirror!"

My brother was sneering in the candlelight; getting closer to me in the darkness. "Wish, Tippi, *wish!*" he said.

The fifth, the sixth: "I wish the Mirrorman would stay in the mirror!"

FX: Something terrible rising...

And then, in the light of the little flame, my brother's face... changed. His smile collapsed in an instant and he looked... frightened.

"Tippi... I can see him, Tippi... I can see him in the mirror!"

The fear in him spread to me. I did not dare turn around.

I lit the candle, blew it out, then lit it again and again and again: "I wish the Mirrorman would stay in the mirror!"

"Tippi! I can see his rotten fingers and his wasted face! He's here! Tippi! Can't you feel him? He's climbing out! He's coming towards me! DO IT! MAKE THE WISH! YOU STUPID, DISGUSTING GIRL!"

TIPPI's expression changes. It's clear that she now wishes for something else.

I picked up my final match. I lit the candle.

I made my final wish... and blew out the flame.

And in that last instant of light, I thought I saw my brother being led away by a most dreadful hand, into the shimmering darkness of the mirror.

MUSIC stops

8.

Tippi's house

TIPPI: When Mother came home, my brother was nowhere to be found.

I had covered every mirror in the house. But Mother was too preoccupied to worry about that.

I told my story about the Mirrorman. The candles. The wishes.

We never saw my brother again.

9.

MUSIC: Mirrorman theme variation

TIPPI: Now, I am an adult. And, of course, I do not believe in such things.

Mother is long gone – she left to stay with her sister, my aunt, who was wealthy and dying. She told me this in a scribbled note. No matter how many letters I wrote to her, she never wrote back.

She left me the house, which was now my own. With my brother gone, everything was mine.

Even that old wooden trunk in the attic, which could only be unlocked from the outside. The one Mother never even knew was there… and so never thought to check…

*

MUSIC: Mirrorman theme

I still keep the mirrors covered. Out of habit, you understand, not superstition. No, I do not believe in such things.

Still… all the same… every year… I dedicate each extinguished flame to the Mirrorman. It's a tradition, that's all. Every family has its traditions.

And each birthday I think to myself: *'Perhaps… this should be the year I claim my wishes back and* wish for something else. Something brighter! Something for myself!'

Perhaps. Perhaps.

MUSIC stops

The final moments play out in silence. TIPPI sits at the table with the covered mirror behind her.

In front of her is a birthday cake with a single candle.

Thirty matches are laid out in a circle. She picks up the first and strikes it.

TIPPI lights the candle. She makes a wish and blows out the candle.

She repeats this several times and then...

TIPPI lights a match. She lights the candle again. She makes a wish and blows out the candle. The cover, at the last moment of light, slips off the mirror as if thrown. (Is that a figure? Standing there with its back to us?)

TIPPI lights a match. She lights the candle again. The mirror is uncovered, but empty. TIPPI makes a wish and blows out the candle.

And then...

TIPPI lights a match. She lights the candle again. She pauses, hesitates. Closes her eyes. Wishes for something new...

In an instant:

TIPPI senses something and turns.

The MIRRORMAN is standing in the mirror, reaching out for TIPPI with his wasted, rotting fingers.

FX: *A shriek, a flicker, a flash, the sound of smashing glass. A scream.*

Blackout

INTERVAL

ACT 3

THE XYLOTHEQUE

1.

The Book of Darkness & Light is centre stage, in a pool of light.

THE MUSICIAN enters. She begins playing a mournful tune.

THE SHADE enters. She picks up the book and inspects it.

THE STORYTELLER enters. He observes THE SHADE.

STORYTELLER/SHADE:

Ours is a life sentence.

We are bound to the book because of our curiosity. We each acted on a fleeting desire to know... and this was the price. Just as a bell cannot be un-rung, forbidden knowledge cannot be given back.

Which brings us to our final tale.

It concerns a house, Willowfield Manor, once owned by a disgraced surgeon named Godfrey Isaiah Leach.

Some said that Leach was in league with the devil. Some asserted that he was a practitioner of witchcraft. Others claimed he conducted the most appalling experiments on human victims – experiments that went against God and nature – that this was the reason for his ex-communication from the medical community.

After Leach's mysterious death, Willowfield Manor stood empty for almost a century; falling into disrepair and dereliction. It retained an evil reputation. Many, in the surrounding villages of Ebbingdon and Fleetford, attested to witnessing repulsive sounds and sights long after Leach was deep in the ground...

Not so very long ago, a decision was made to raze and the rebuild the Willowfield Estate in its entirety. In the Spring of that same year, Dr Esther Blackwood, Chief Archivist at the Nesbit National Library, was tasked with surveying, cataloguing and recovering the rare books in Leach's infamous collection.

The following tale takes the form of a first-hand account by Dr Blackwood, detailing her experiences on that fateful expedition.

2.

MUSIC: The dream theme

THE STORYTELLER and THE SHADE become DR ESTHER BLACKWOOD.

The dream

FX: Nightmarish tones and sounds

ESTHER: The night before I went to Willowfield, I had the dream again. It always goes the same way...

I am in a large, dark room with two great skylights above. A waning, yellow moon, is visible through the dusty glass.

I am bound to a wooden chair; tight straps cut savagely into my skin. The walls are in darkness. Beside me is a table on which a black candle burns. The wax drips and collects into a hideous pool, which stinks like the pit of a pulled rotten tooth.

Something is screaming in the next room.

FX: *Screams from the next room, inhuman*

I sense... a face. Twisted and scowling and hateful. A man with dead, steel-coloured eyes. He is speaking to me:

VOICE: Take it! Pass it along! Bring it to the world!

ESTHER: A horrible pain nags at me, now. On my forearm are several, tiny open wounds. And from these lesions, suddenly... black-green shoots begin to sprout. They grow thicker and rougher as they push out of my flesh; dragging veins and muscle with them.

Now, I am conscious of hot, foul breath on my neck and then two great and terrible arms grab me...!

Two arms, as described, grab ESTHER.

MUSIC: *Shriek*

Lights drop out and then come back in.

ESTHER wakes, suddenly.

> I woke in the safety of my room.
>
> How real it seemed, this time.
>
> I can feel those dreadful shoots, still.

3.

Ebbingdon

MUSIC: *Xylotheque theme*

FX: *Train arriving, leaving. A low wind*

ESTHER: It was almost dark when I arrived at Ebbingdon station.

Digs had been arranged for me – a cottage on the edge of the Willowfield Estate, owned by the caretaker and groundskeeper, a Mr Vaughan Tallent. I had assumed that Mr Tallent would meet me at the station, but there was no sign of him.

A local man helped me with my things. I offered him a few pounds and he agreed to drive me to the digs. But when I handed over the address, the man appeared to change his mind quite suddenly. With few other options, I pleaded with him to reconsider, and told him that I could pay double what I'd already offered. Eventually, he relented.

When we got to the cottage, and my new companion had helped me unload my bags, I noticed that he could hardly take his eyes off the dramatic silhouette cast by Willowfield Manor.

I tried to pay him for the lift... but he would not take my money. And in the next moment, he took hold of my shoulders and said: "May the Lord keep you safe."

With this, he climbed back into his vehicle and drove away into the night. Quite strange.

Local superstitions are alive and well in this part of the world, it seems.

ESTHER tries to dismiss this with a laugh, but cannot.

4.

Mr Tallent's cottage

MUSIC: *Unsettling chords, slow*

On the front door of the cottage is a note. ESTHER takes it down and reads it

TALLENT: *(VOICE) Dear Dr. Blackwood. The door is on the latch. There's soup and bread and tea on the table. I'm always early-to-bed and sleep like the dead. Your room is made up for you and there's a small fire in the grate - it can get a little chilly.*

Yours

V. Tallent.

5.

The following morning.

Willowfield Manor

MUSIC: *Willowfield theme*

ESTHER: My first morning at Willowfield began with a breakfast of weak coffee and over-salted porridge, prepared by Mr Tallent. He told me that he lived alone - except for his old Collie, Bess – and had done for many years. He seemed, frankly, perturbed and rather put out to have me.

            After I'd eaten, Mr Tallent mumbled an offer to walk up to the Manor House with me and show me around the site. We strolled up together, with Bess waddling along beside us.

FX: *Bess panting and barking occasionally*

TALLENT: I'll warn you, it's quite a circus up there. There's people surveying the land, the trees, clearing the rooms, digging up the ground. That's progress, is it? Fifty years I've minded this place. And my old dad kept it fifty before that. Never seen so many people poking about. If they were wise, they'd just get on and pull it down. And I won't be sorry when they do.

ESTHER: "Has it always been empty, the Manor?" I asked. "For as long as you've been here, I mean?"

TALLENT: After old Dr. Leach... people didn't want to go near it.

ESTHER: I thought of the man who had driven me from the station.

"Ah yes, Dr Leach. I did try to read up on him. There was hardly anything of fact. The only thing I could find was some sordid little tabloid story about him being struck off for conducting illegal experiments! And his death certificate, of course. 'Undetermined' circumstances."

TALLENT: Mm. Well. There's a lot of stories about Leach.

ESTHER: "Perhaps you might be able to share some with me, while I'm staying here?"

TALLENT: (*Looks at her. Ignores her request*) Here we are, then.

They arrive at the house.

6.

Outside the Manor

FX: *Wind in the trees. Workers milling about*

ESTHER: The Manor was a sorry sight. The walls looked brittle; the remaining glass panes precarious in the splintering frames. Ivy snaked across much of exterior and vines were bursting out of innumerable cracks and fissures.

There was, indeed, a hive of activity around the place. Mr Tallent excused himself for a moment to check in with some of the workers.

A removal team were carrying out a large, wide shelving unit covered with a dust sheet. It took three of them to manage the thing and even then it was, evidently, a struggle.

They stumbled. A sealed jar fell from under the sheet and smashed on the floor.

FX: Stumble, smash

An oily-looking liquid and something beige and soft-looking slopped out. The men looked down with disgust, covering their mouths and noses. Eventually, one of them was elected to clear up the mess.

ESTHER looks around

Mr Tallent was now talking to a man in overalls. They were standing in the shade of an enormous, stout yew tree.

FX: The creaking tree

MUSIC: The yew theme

What a fearful thing the tree was! Quite hellish. Strange shapes were present in the gnarled bark – not unlike human faces. Mouths agape, eyes wide, torn features. I found I kept having to suppress a shudder each time I looked at it.

*FX: **Bess crying softly***

Bess, the old collie, was pacing anxiously next to her owner.

The man in overalls wore an expression of grave concern. He produced what appeared to be a rather tatty, slim book. Its leather cover was smeared in soil and garden detritus.

The man pointed at the roots of the tree. I stepped a little closer. "We found it in there," he said.

He handed the book to Mr Tallent. In the same moment, Bess bolted; scampering, frenziedly, towards me.

*FX: **Bess yelping and barking***

She sheltered behind me. I reached down and patted her, feeling her cry deeply.

Mr Tallent, watching Bess go, calmly put the book into his satchel and walked over to join me once more.

7.

TALLENT: Daft dog. Scared of her own shadow. Sorry about that. Mr Samuels, there, and his team have some reservations about the old yew tree. Can't pull it down till they know the full picture. Looking for life, inside and out.

ESTHER: I looked up at the tree. Its branches were barren of birds.

"And have they found any? Life?"

TALLENT: (*Mumbles*) Not exactly.

ESTHER reacts and tries to ask more questions. TALLENT gestures towards the house.

We should press on. I've a busy morning.

ESTHER: As we walked up the steps to the house, with our backs to the tree, I could not suppress the peculiar impression that I was being watched.

MUSIC: *Unnerving melody*

I had what I can only describe as an *awareness* that some creature, roosting in the lower limbs, was observing us. Absurd, of course, and all it took was a glance over my shoulder to confirm what nonsense I was entertaining. Nevertheless, try as I might, I couldn't shake the uneasy feeling.

8.

Inside the Manor

ESTHER: The inside of the Manor was in a worse state than the decaying façade. The floorboards were riddled with treacherous holes; numerous cracks in the plaster revealed crumbling brickwork; twigs and dead leaves littered the foyer.

We made our way up the staircase, to the very top floor, and along a wide corridor, at the end of which were two doors. One stood open to the room beyond. The other was closed.

FX: *A growing sense of unease*

TALLENT: Through here.

ESTHER: Mr Tallent led on into the open room. Before I followed, I was dragged by my curiosity to try the second door. It was locked. I tried to shoulder it, in case it was merely swollen in the frame. It did not budge an inch.

Mr Tallent turned back towards me. He gave me a stern look of warning.

"Will they be clearing this room, too? I'd hate to miss anything. I understand Leach's collection is quite extensive."

TALLENT: You'll be long gone before they get in that room. Besides, there's no books in there.

ESTHER and TALLENT exchange an awkward glance.

ESTHER walks into the library.

9.

The library

MUSIC: The library theme

FX: A low hum

ESTHER: The old library was vast and decrepit. Scores of shelves lined the walls, all crammed with books, some buckling under the weight. Dozens more editions were piled high on the floor or scattered into corners.

There was a tremendous, overpowering smell of mould in the air, which led me to wonder how much of the collection could be salvaged.

There was something unsettling and familiar about the room, the significance of which did not immediately come to mind.

And then I glanced upwards.

And I realised where I was...

FX: Nightmarish tones

MUSIC: The dream theme

Two great, dusty skylights dominated the ceiling. This was the room from my dream! It was identical in almost every way, except for the absence of that dreadful chair and wretched candle...

VOICE: Take it! Pass it along! Bring it to the world!

MUSIC stops

ESTHER: *I must have seen photographs* – I told myself. But how long had I been plagued by that same dream? It felt like years...

TALLENT: Are you well? Only, you look rather pale...

ESTHER: "I'm fine. If it's alright, I'll begin. There's a lot to get through."

TALLENT: If I were you, I'd throw the lot on a bonfire. If he touched it... burn it. Never liked this room. 'Mon Bess.... Bess... Bess, come on!

ESTHER: The dog had hardly moved from my side since her turn by the old yew.

"You can leave her, if you like? The company would be nice."

Mr Tallent shrugged.

TALLENT: I'll be back to walk her later, then. Be good, dog.

TALLENT exits.

ESTHER looks at the shelves.

ESTHER: "Right then, Bess. Where to begin?"

10.

The library

ESTHER is inspecting the bookshelves.

ESTHER: There were some gems within the collection: an early Rothschild Prayerbook, various rare translations of the four gospels, and, perhaps most impressively, a second edition of The Northumberland Bestiary.

Leach had amassed, too, a great many books on botany, dendrology and, somewhat intriguingly, joinery. There were medical textbooks aplenty; titles on anatomy and surgery – all annotated beyond further use.

None of this, however, was as intriguing as the vast array of books on the occult. Here was Beauchamp on The Witch Trials of the 17th Century; Witt on the Uses of Satanic Runes; even Muncer's epic tome on The Palladists.

When I spotted this latter publication (the rarest of the lot), I pulled it carelessly from the pile, bringing the rest of the books down with it.

FX: *Low, peculiar tone*

A strange red-orange box is visible

Behind the fallen tower, a small cabinet was revealed. It was constructed from a dark-orange wood and was covered with a thick layer of dust.

There was a little latch on the front. Reaching around the mound of texts, I was able to flick it open and draw back a sliding door. It stuck almost immediately but I could see, inside, the spine of a particularly old-looking book.

In its buried state, the cabinet was impossible to get at.

"That'll be a treat for later, then," I said. "Time for a tea break, eh Bess..?"

FX: *Bess growls*

The dog was rigid with agitation. Her lip was curled back in a snarl. She was looking at the cabinet.

"What is it?" I asked, hopelessly. I could see nothing that might be the matter.

"Come on, Bess. It's alright. Just a silly old box."

It took quite some time to settle her.

ESTHER goes to the window.

I stood a while at the window, admiring the rare Muncer edition. Again, the pages were annotated heavily – raising doubt of the Nesbit Library making any use of it.

*MUSIC: **The yew theme***

Outside, Mr Samuels was at the top of his ladder, working away on the yew tree. He had a T-shaped tool with which he was boring into the trunk. Bark cracked and fell away, exposing the heartwood beneath.

*FX: **Sound of the yew creaking and groaning***

It was a strange deep-orange colour, exactly matching the cabinet I had discovered earlier...

And then the most extraordinary thing happened. As Mr Samuels bored further into the tree, a cloud blackish liquid exploded out of the puncture; it resembled a dense mist of tiny insects.

FX: *A wet explosion*

Mr Samuels slipped off the top rung and slid down the ladder; landing awkwardly at the bottom. He struggled to his knees, doubled over and vomited, violently.

His colleagues were soon at his side, offering help. They got him to his feet and led him away.

ESTHER looks over at the cabinet.

MUSIC stops

FX: *Creaking, damp, organic sounds*

VOICE: (*Whispered*) Take it. Pass it along. Bring it to the world.

11.

Willowfield estate/ The old cemetery

MUSIC: *Willowfield theme*

FX: *A chill wind*

ESTHER: I decided on a walk before returning to the cottage that first evening. I hoped the fresh air would rid me of that dreadful, lingering smell of mould. Bess and I plodded slowly up the winding path to the top of the hill that loomed behind the Manor.

There, I discovered an old cemetery. The site was untended and woefully overgrown - subsidence abound - and there were a great many unmarked graves. A melancholy place. But I found sitting with Bess and sipping my leftover tea quite peaceful. It was a treat to be able to take in the whole of Willowfield and the valley that winds down into Ebbingdon, Fleetford and beyond.

MUSIC stops

There is a growing sense that several, deathly figures are approaching ESTHER from behind.

And there was the Manor, dominating the view.

The dusk light had a shimmering quality to it. It must have affected my vision because, for a lingering moment, I thought I saw a pale face peering back at me from one of the windows on the upper floor.

MUSIC: Menacing, haunting

This, of course, was not strange in and of itself... except for one fact: the window belonged to the locked room. I knew this even from my limited knowledge of the house.

FX: Deathly, creeping sounds

The vision was not quite solid; rather, it had the immaterial quality of a reflection. The face was strangely elongated and the mouth seemed to hang slackly open. I blinked, hard, but the vision remained...

ESTHER stands, shades her eyes for a clearer look. She is startled by TALLENT, who suddenly appears behind her.

TALLENT: *(Loud)* This is where you got to, is it?

ESTHER: "Mr Tallent. Look – in that room... the locked room... there's somebody staring..."

But, when I looked again, the window was quite empty. The sun had dropped a little way and the light was no longer dazzling.

ESTHER can't believe it was merely a mirage.

TALLENT: Seeing spooks, are ya? *(Pause)* There's supper at the cottage if you want it. C'mon Bess.

12.

The library

ESTHER: On the next day, as I returned to the library, I was compelled to check the door of the locked room again.

ESTHER checks the locked door.

The knowledge that I would most likely never discover what was in there was maddening.

I spent the entire morning dutifully cataloguing and sorting those books which might be of value to the Nesbit Library.

ESTHER slides the cabinet out.

*MUSIC: **The library theme, variation***

*FX: **Ominous tones, grow***

Early in the afternoon, I turned my attention to the wooden cabinet I had found the day before. Having cleared away the books obscuring it, I dragged it to the centre of the room and heaved it onto a table.

I flicked open the latch. This time, I was able to slide back the cabinet door fully. Inside was a row of what appeared, at first, to be unremarkable antiquarian books. A closer look revealed the truth.

These were not books at all... but seven boxes crafted to *resemble* books. They were beautifully sculpted from wood.

My heart all-but stopped. This was a xylotheque.

*MUSIC: **The Xylotheque theme***

I had read about them before, but had never actually seen one in the flesh, as it were.

A xylotheque is – in essence – a collection of wood specimens. Each volume is made from the timber of a specific species. Inside each box – I knew – would be dried cuttings from those same species. Leaves, seeds, flowers and so on. It is, simply, an ornate way of cataloguing trees.

But xylotheques of this age and condition are extremely rare. I wondered at its value. Surely this was the jewel in the crown of Leach's collection.

Taking great care, I inspected the volumes.

ESTHER lines up the books.

Years of neglect had led to an accumulation of dirt and grease, which made the labels on the spines impossible to read. Each "book" was bound around with black twine. They looked like they hadn't been opened for many decades.

I took out the final volume and was about to untie the twine, when it occurred to check that no other treasures remained in the cabinet.

ESTHER gets on her knees and inspects the case.

I plunged my hand inside and felt around.

She reaches inside.

MUSIC stops

FX: *A crawling, organic sound, like insects in the eardrums*

At first, I found nothing. But then... my fingertips glanced over something tucked deep into one corner. It was cold and clammy to the touch; in texture it was not unlike the surface of an earthworm.

And then, with alarming quickness... whatever it was moved, sweeping odiously across my fingers. I had the most terrible sensation of being stroked...

I jerked my hand out, fast...

ESTHER cries out. Blood spurts from wounds on her arm.

MUSIC: Shrill, single note

FX: Mangled, deep, guttural laughter

The rough panelling of the cabinet delivered a ribbon of splinters to my forearm. I went, quickly, to the window to see the extent of the damage.

ESTHER inspects her injury. She takes out a handkerchief and dabs the wounds. She starts to pick out the splinters. Finally, she then tears a strip of fabric from the packing materials and winds it around her arm.

Mr Tallent stumbled into the room in great haste.

TALLENT: I heard a scream...

ESTHER: "Oh yes. It was just..."

I looked over at the table, expecting there to be a mess of spattered blood.

But there was nothing.

Neither on the volumes of the xylotheque nor the cabinet.

ESTHER looks incredulous. She looks at her covered arm. Presses it and winces.

> "I... I saw a rat. I hate them."

TALLENT: A rat. You must have been unlucky. I've never seen one up here...

ESTHER: (*Looking towards the case*). "I'm actually feeling a little unwell, Mr Tallent. All this dust, I suppose. I think I'll walk back with you."

> I looked at the cabinet once more. *Surely just mould or fungus. Or perhaps a large insect...*
>
> But a vile, stubborn thought kept resurfacing:
>
> No.
>
> The thing that had touched me...
>
> It was a hand.
>
> They were fingers.

ESTHER packs the Xylotheque away and locks the cabinet.

MUSIC: The library theme, variation

> As we descended the staircase, with my arm now beginning to throb, I happened to glance at the locked door. And, a moment before it went out of sight, I could have sworn that I saw an infinitesimal movement of the door handle...

13.

Walking to the cottage

ESTHER occasionally winces as her arm gives her pain.

FX: Creaking of trees, wind.

ESTHER: On the way back to the cottage, we passed by the old yew tree.

There was a most foul odour on the air. Something rich, deep and sour.

FX: Bess barks and howls

Bess scampered past the tree, giving it the widest possible berth.

"What is it about the yew tree?" I asked Mr Tallent. "Why doesn't she like it?"

TALLENT: She's daft as a brush, that's why.

ESTHER: I explained what I had seen the previous day; the incident with Mr Samuels. I drew attention to the terrible smell on the air; which was worsening the closer we got to the tree.

"Perhaps Bess can... I don't know... *sense* something..."

TALLENT: I thought you were an academic! You sound as mad as the folk in Ebbingdon. Amount of stories I've heard about that tree over the years. If I had a pound for each of 'em. Magic and nonsense.

ESTHER: "Well if it's nonsense, there's no harm in telling me, is there?"

TALLENT: You're very curious. Don't you know what becomes of the curious? (*Regards her. Then, reluctantly*) Round here, people call that the Corpse Tree. They say it's fed by 'dead water'. You see how the land forms a valley down from Monk Hill? When it *rains*, you see, all that water soaks through the ground. Through the graves. Through what's inside. Gathering up what it gathers up, seeping down into the soil. Feeding the tree. They say it's infected with the dead.

But, there again, the same folk'll tell you that Leach held Black Masses under that yew. That he was some sort of necromancer. Soft-headed fools! I think they enjoy playing at scaring themselves!

FX: A strange whisper on the wind

ESTHER: "The man who drove me from the station - he was *afraid*. It wasn't an act. Leach's reputation must have come from somewhere..."

ESTHER stares at him, unrelenting. TALLENT continues...

TALLENT: That it did. (*Pause. Sighs, reluctantly continues*)

Years ago, when Leach was alive, a good many people went missing from their beds in Ebbingdon and Fleetford. Kidnapped, people said. Though no-one saw anyone coming or going. They blamed Leach. Said he was using them in his experiments. They said he *started* by robbing graves, up there on Monk Hill. But that he came to prefer fresher specimens. But it's all just tall tales.

ESTHER: "And you don't believe them."

TALLENT: I believed 'em as a boy. But boys are stupid. Now? (*He shakes his head*) Leach was a wrong'un, there's no doubting that. But necromancy? Bringing folk back to life...?

ESTHER: A strange smile crossed Mr Tallent's lips.

MUSIC: Unnerving, tense, unsettling

FX: Blood, bone, root, bark

TALLENT: The story that always scared me, and it was the one I heard most of all, was that Leach was *making* something in that Manor house. Using parts of those missing people. And parts of that Corpse Tree. Splicing two sorts of life... to create something that could not die. Something of blood and bone and root and bark. Only, they said, whatever he created – it turned on him. Tore him too pieces. He didn't listen to the warnings of his peers, ignored the experts. He believed he was right and he stopped at nothing to prove it to the world. And he got his comeuppance.

My dad used to say to me: 'Don't play near the Manor or Old Leach will drag you inside and turn you into something rotten. And, whatever you do, don't go near that Corpse Tree. One splinter, son... one splinter...' He repeated that warning often. But he never finished the sentence. And I was always glad. (*Weak laugh*) Nonsense!

ESTHER: (*She holds her arm and looks concerned*). I felt a sudden, painful twinge in my arm.

FX: *The agony of the injury*

TALLENT: What have you done there?

ESTHER: "Must have pulled something moving the books. I'm quite alright."

A large cloud crawled across the sun.

The stench on the air had dispersed now. It was only after it had gone that I recognised the foul odour.

It was the smell of maggots.

MUSIC: *Unnerving, tense, unsettling*

MUSIC stops

14.

The cottage

ESTHER: When we reached the cottage, Mr Tallent and Bess continued on into the village with some errands to run. I was glad of the solitude.

I removed the remaining splinters from my arm and bathed the cuts. Though small, they hurt badly. Ached from the inside.

Thoughts of the xylotheque, of that odious thing within the cabinet, of Leach, of the Corpse Tree, all writhed in my head. I found myself pacing back and forth, unable to get my mind in order. I poured a small measure of scotch and sat by the fire a while.

Next to me was a side table. On it, under a stack of invoices, letters and receipts, a small patch of dark leather was visible.

ESTHER moves the papers and produces the book.

MUSIC: The yew theme

It was the book that Samuels had passed to Mr Tallent. The one he had found in the roots of the yew tree. Similarly to the volumes of the xylotheque, I saw that it, too, was bound around with black twine.

ESTHER takes off the twine, opens the book and begins to read.

The pages were handwritten and became less and less legible with each entry. There were diagrams – anatomical sketches, along with drawings of flowers and trees. There was the odd clipping here and there, and photographs that had faded dreadfully with time.

Here was a list of words in latin: *Cutis, Vesica et Ren… Ventri et Alvum.* They rang the faintest bell somewhere in my head.

ESTHER reads a few entries, flicking through the pages randomly. As she does so, she becomes less and less comfortable.

I wiped the dirt away from the cover and saw that three initials were embossed there:

G.I.L.

15.

LEACH's journal

MUSIC: Agitated and urgent

ESTHER/LEACH: "I have found the finest specimens. Signs of movement and life."

"The thing's strength dips and rises violently. It thrives at night."

"Those fools in London know nothing. They do not understand what I am on the cusp of discovering."

ESTHER's arm begins to bother her.

"The creation is ailing. I am working tirelessly... Cursed God! How it seems to suffer..."

ESTHER scratches at her bandaged arm.

"It died this morning on the table. I will catalogue the progress. Make a show if its terrible beauty. It must be passed along! (*ESTHER pauses at this – these are the words from her dream*).

95

"Its death will not be for nothing. I have wept often today – am I not a grieving father?"

*

ESTHER flicks through the pages. Her arm is itching terribly.

"Xylotheque...

xylotheque...

xylotheque...

xylotheque..."

ESTHER's arm is too much for her to bear. She takes the bandage off. The wounds are dark and worrying. Something is spreading within her. She re-wraps the wound and exits.

FX: Writing and creeping

MUSIC stops

16.

ESTHER's bedroom

MUSIC: New nightmare theme

ESTHER: That night I had a new dream. In it, I saw a journey to the Manor house under a black sky and a stark moon. I sensed that same cruel face again; those dead, steel-coloured eyes. I felt his voice.

VOICE: "Take it! Pass it along! Bring it to the world!"

ESTHER: I saw the stag-headed yew tree.

I saw myself entering the Manor.

I saw forgotten basement rooms. Beetles and worms and dust and filth.

*FX: **Wood creaking, bottles clinking, insects scuttling***

I saw the attic library; books and blood. Those horned-skylights allowing in a grim light.

And then I saw the locked room. I saw its door creak open. I saw myself go in. I saw shelves of jars and matter inside: leaves and stems, organs and flesh floating in greasy water. Black candles on the walls, upside down yet somehow burning.

I saw implements; rusted and treacherous; clotted with gore.

I saw a wooden bed with brown-red stained sawdust beneath. An operating table.

I saw a figure upon it. And that face leering over. Those cruel, dead eyes.

*FX: **The creation***

The smell of maggots. Cultures from the yew tree meeting skin; invading flesh; melding with bone.

The creature on the table began to rise...

Pause.

97

FX: The creation cries out in pain; a horrible, agonised, hateful scream

ESTHER suddenly jerks awake, gasping for air. She clutches her wounded arm.

Blackout

VOICE: (*Whispered*) Take it. Pass it along. Bring it to the world.

17.

Lights up

The library

ESTHER packs away books. She looks noticeably ill. She is sweating and her arm is bothering her greatly. The wound is weeping through the bandage. She shivers occasionally.

She unravels the bandage. Small shoots are beginning to sprout from her arm. Horrified, she produces some nail scissors and trims them before covering up the wounds again. She pretends it is not happening.

ESTHER: My final day at Willowfield was a Sunday. The entire Manor was empty and quiet. Along with Mr Tallent, who had agreed to assist me, I spent the morning packing books into boxes ready to be collected the following day.

I had put the cabinet containing the xylotheque to one side.

TALLENT: (*Looking at the cabinet*) What about this?

MUSIC: Sombre and mournful

ESTHER: There was a peculiar look on Mr Tallent's face as he regarded the cabinet.

"I'll be taking it personally. It's rather… delicate."

TALLENT: You know what I think. Should've burned the lot.

ESTHER: "Yes, thank you Mr Tallent. But I'm afraid that is not your decision. This now belongs to me… to the Nesbit Library."

TALLENT: Are you sure you're alright, Dr. Blackwood?

ESTHER: "Please stop fussing, Mr Tallent. If you'd like to be of help, you could carry that cabinet back to the cottage for me."

TALLENT: If it's all the same to you, I'd rather not touch it. C'mon Bess.

FX: Bess panting, crying. Footsteps

ESTHER: Mr Tallent left without another word.

I did a final recce of the library then, once satisfied, picked up the xylotheque cabinet. It was very painful to do so – it seemed impossibly heavy in my arms.

MUSIC stops

As I descending the staircase for the final time, my eye was drawn, again, to the locked door.

FX: *Something lurking behind the door, strange breathing*

Only this time...

...it was open.

I stared hard at the gap between door and frame and was certain I saw movement in the darkness beyond.

FX: *Something squirms and hides away*

I hurried down the stairs and left the house as quickly as I could.

The journey to the cottage was a dreadful struggle. I did not look back at the Manor house once.

18.

The cottage, ESTHER's bedroom

A fire is blazing

ESTHER: Back in my room, I built a small but warming fire to stop my shivering.

My compulsion to examine the xylotheque was overwhelming. Something was drawing me to it; just as something had compelled me to take it from the house in the first place.

ESTHER unpacks the volumes, wary of the treacherous cabinet

I emptied the cabinet carefully onto the desk and lined up the seven volumes. I cut away the black twine that bound each closed. I opened the first book.

ESTHER unties the black twine and opens the volume.

MUSIC: The Xylotheque theme, slower

Inside were samples, as I had anticipated.

But not the kind I might have expected. Not leaves, grasses or seeds. What was in the box more resembled thin sheets of pale leather. The smell that emanated from inside was that of chemicals and rot.

FX: Something strange is growing

ESTHER rubs away the grime on the spine of a volume and reads the label:

"*Cutis.*"

I turned my attention to the other boxes, wiping away the grease on their spines.

ESTHER does this in turn and reads the words. She does this increasingly frantically.

"*Vesica et Ren.*"

I felt something grow cold in my bones...

"*Ventri et Alvum.*"

These samples...

"Pulmo et Iecur."

None of them were from plants or trees...

"Oculus et Capillum."

Oh God...!

ESTHER picks up the penultimate box.

"Dentes."

As she turns the box, the sound of teeth rattling against wood can be heard.

ESTHER, panicking now, raging against the thing that is starting to take control of her, picks up and starts to read through Leach's journal again, looking for answers.

ESTHER/LEACH: *Reading from Leach's diary*

As she reads, LEACH's influence and voice seems to grow stronger in her.

MUSIC: Urgent, frantic

"I have catalogued its essence, its organs. They are unique. They must be preserved for further study. The carcass I shall commit to the earth."

"The grave is disturbed! Six weeks in the ground! And I have taken every vital thing from it! How does it yet live?"

"I shall hide my work, I shall bury this journal... My best hope is that someone will find it. Take it. Pass it along. Bring it to the world."

> "Dreadful Hell! I have seen it tonight! It is returned! It is coming to the house…!"

ESTHER throws the book down.

She retrieves the final box in the xylotheque.

ESTHER: *"Cor."*

MUSIC: Tense

She opens the wooden volume, slowly reaches in and produces a desiccated humanesque heart. She holds it out in front of her.

She stares at it, consumed with horror.

The heart beats in her hand.

ESTHER screams out, drops the heart into the box and slams it closed.

> A surge of fresh horror was upon me now. I needed to be away from the wretched thing!

ESTHER runs from the room.

19.

On the landing

MUSIC: Chaotic, frantic, danger growing

ESTHER: The moment I stepped onto the landing I was arrested by a disgusting odour. Hot and thick and rising. The smell of corruption.

I crept forwards and peered over the bannisters.

And what I saw, upon the stair, was an inconceivable horror.

It had followed me from the Manor.

FX: The creation approaches. It creaks and groans and growls, it slouches and squelches and slobbers and scuttles

Skin like timber; finger-tips, torn, wooden bones protruding, sharp as if carved. Arms long, like branches; twisted. Dislocated. The chest: wide open, peeled, revealing a dark, empty pit. The face, potted with holes; like honeycomb or worm-infested wood with one, rheumy yellow eye, glinting dully from a deep socket.

It seemed to half-walk, half-scuttle up the stairs towards me, like an insect.

As it moved upwards, it groaned. I could feel it through the landing.

I felt a presence inside my head. A face. A voice.

VOICE: (*Shouting*) "Take it! Pass it along! Bring it to the world!"

ESTHER: My arm screamed with pain; molten metal burned in my veins.

She reaches out towards the creature, no longer in control of her arm.

FX: The creation cries out in rage

And then the abominable thing on the stairs turned its horrible eye upon me and lunged with such sudden violence that I fell backwards, against the door and into my room once more.

*

I slammed the door and pushed the bolt home just in time.

The door began to rupture in its frame...

The hinges started to give; the wood began to splinter...

The thing's getting inside was inevitable... and in those desperate moments, a wild idea seized me.

I ran across the room and picked up as many of the volumes of the xylotheque as I could manage and quickly piled them onto the fire – each volume exciting the flames. Even as I did this, I felt an agonising protest in my head; in my body.

ESTHER piles the xylotheque onto the fire.

Those steel-coloured eyes! That voice!

VOICE: *No! Take it, pass it along!*

ESTHER: Screaming, now!

My hands burnt, my arm an agony, my eyes blinded by brown smoke, I piled the volumes on.

Behind me, I felt a fearful, violent movement of air and knew that the door had given way.

I picked up the last of the volumes, the one containing that dreadful heart... And pushed it into the flames.

A wretched cry emanated from within me. It seemed to tear through the fabric of the house...

...and when I felt a hand take hold of my shoulder, I grabbed the iron poker at the side of the fireplace, wheeled around and thrust...

ESTHER turns and stabs.

There stood Mr Tallent; eyes wide, mouth agape and slack, the fresh wound in his stomach swallowing the poker.

ESTHER pulls out the poker. TALLENT falls to his knees.

Bess paced and barked by the fractured and splintered door. And, so far as I could see, there was nothing else at all.

FX: Bess cries and yelps

ESTHER picks up LEACH's diary.

She exits apace.

20.

MUSIC: The Xylotheque theme

STORYTELLER/SHADE:

It was the fire that summoned the villagers. They saw the sky filled with smoke and the cottage violently ablaze.

Once there, they found and followed a frantic old sheepdog. She led them to the bank of the Ebbing River, close to the burning cottage. Here they discovered the old groundskeeper, Mr Tallent. Gravely wounded, free from the flames... alive.

When they asked him what had happened, who had inflicted this terrible injury upon him, the old man could only murmur incoherently and gesture, vaguely, towards Willowfield Manor.

MUSIC stops

21.

MUSIC: **Slow, melancholy**

STORYTELLER/SHADE:

As for Dr. Esther Blackwood, there are no records that fully explain her fate... save for a single account, given by a railway worker.

On the night of that fateful fire, the young man reported assisting an ill-looking woman into her carriage.

Under her right arm, so the lad reported, she was carrying a leather-bound book. Something in her actions indicated that the old, tattered thing was extremely precious to her and she behaved jealously about it.

The woman's other arm dangled uselessly at her side, as though it were badly wounded. "You could see the pain of it in her face," the young man said. He noted that, as he left her alone in the carriage, the smell of rot was thick in the air.

But the strangest thing - so the lad claimed - was that as the train pulled away, he caught sight of the woman in her carriage again. Only now she wasn't alone.

At her side sat a man.

FX: Something sinister grows...

"He seemed to be whispering to her," the lad said. "He was evil-looking. And his eyes. There was something about his eyes. Fixed, dead. The colour of steel."

FX: Train leaving the station

MUSIC stops

EPILOGUE

MUSIC: Upon the Stair theme

THE STORYTELLER picks up The Book of Darkness & Light.

STORYTELLER/SHADE:

And so our time here draws to a close. And our next journey opens up before us.

If you have discovered lessons in these tales, we hope they will be well observed. If not, we can hardly help it.

Go, then, back to the safety of your homes. But have a care, now, not to dismiss that strange sensation of an unseen presence in the dead of night; that peculiar shape, glanced just for an instant, in the mirror's reflection; that slouching shadow in the tail of your eye. The book has you now.

You are free to leave. But you do not leave free.

You were warned.

Oh yes.

We will see you again.

Your story is just beginning.

THE SHADE approaches THE STORYTELLER. He holds the book up.

THE SHADE reaches for the pages. They open.

FX: Something monstrous is released

Blackout

FX: A blood-curdling scream

CURTAIN

Also by Adam Z. Robinson
from Playdead Press

The Book of Darkness & Light

Shivers